Saturn

Uranus   Neptune

Neptune
and the
Distant Dwarf Planets

Editor in chief: Paul A. Kobasa
Supplementary Publications: Jeff De La Rosa,
    Christine Sullivan, Scott Thomas, Kristina Vaicikonis,
    Marty Zwikel
Research: Mike Barr, Cheryl Graham, Jacqueline Jasek,
    Barbara Lightner, Loranne Shields
Graphics and Design: Kathy Creech, Sandra Dyrlund,
    Tom Evans, Isaiah Sheppard, Brenda Tropinski
Permissions: Janet Peterson
Indexing: David Pofelski
Pre-Press and Manufacturing: Carma Fazio, Anne Fritzinger,
    Steven Hueppchen, Tina Ramirez
Writer: Robert N. Knight

2007 revised printing

World Book, Inc.
233 N. Michigan Avenue
Chicago, IL 60601
U.S.A.

The Library of Congress has cataloged an earlier printing of
this title as follows:
Neptune and the distant dwarf planets. -- 2nd ed.
    p. cm. -- (World Book's solar system & space exploration
library)
    Summary: "Introduction to Neptune and the distant dwarf
planets, providing to primary and intermediate grade students
information on their features and exploration. Includes fun
facts, glossary, resource list and index"--Provided by publisher.
    Includes bibliographical references and index.
    ISBN-13: 978-0-7166-9518-9
    ISBN-10: 0-7166-9518-9
    1. Neptune (Planet)--Juvenile literature. 2. Pluto (Planet)--
Juvenile literature. 3. Outer planets--Juvenile literature.
I. World Book, Inc.
QB691.N44 2007
523.48--dc22   2006030044

This printing:
ISBN: 978-0-7166-9529-5 (Neptune and the Distant Dwarf
        Planets)
ISBN: 978-0-7166-9522-6 (set)

Printed in China

2 3 4 5 6 7 8 09 08 07

For information about other World Book publications,
visit our Web site at http://www.worldbookonline.com or call
1-800-WORLDBK (967-5325).

For information about sales to schools and libraries,
call 1-800-975-3250 (United States);
1-800-837-5365 (Canada).

Picture Acknowledgments: Back Cover: NASA; © Calvin J. Hamilton; NASA; Johns Hopkins University
Applied Physics Laboratory/Southwest Research Institute; Inside Back Cover: © John Gleason, Celestial Images.

© Vanni/Art Resource 29; © Calvin J. Hamilton 13, 61; Johns Hopkins University Applied Physics
Laboratory/Southwest Research Institute 51; Lunar and Planetary Institute 41; NASA 11, 15, 25, 33; NASA/
ESA, and A. Schaller (for STScI) 53; NASA/ESA, H. Weaver (JHU/APL), A. Stern (SwRI), and the HST Pluto
Companion Search Team 47; NASA/JPL 23; NASA/JPL/Caltech 59; NASA, L. Sromovsky, and P. Fry, University
of Wisconsin-Madison 17; © SPL/Photo Researchers 49; © Chris Butler, Photo Researchers 35, 43, 55;
© David A. Hardy, SPL/Photo Researchers 27; W. M. Keck Observatory 57.

Illustrations: Inside Front Cover: WORLD BOOK illustration by Steve Karp; Front Cover & 1, 3, 9, 21, 39, 45,
55: WORLD BOOK illustrations by Paul Perreault; WORLD BOOK illustrations by Precision Graphics 7, 35;
WORLD BOOK illustration 31.

Astronomers use different kinds of photos to learn about objects in space—such as planets. Many photos show
an object's natural color. Other photos use false colors. Some false-color images show types of light the human
eye cannot normally see. Others have colors that were changed to highlight important features. When
appropriate, the captions in this book state whether a photo uses natural or false color.

WORLD BOOK'S

SOLAR SYSTEM & SPACE EXPLORATION LIBRARY

Neptune
and the
Distant Dwarf Planets

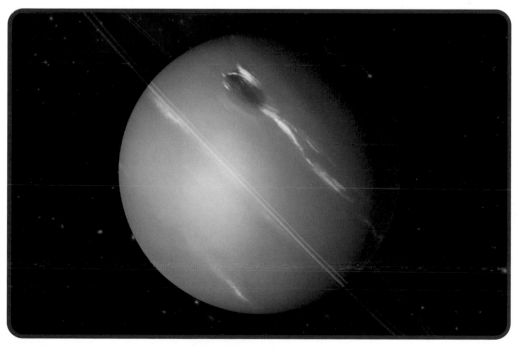

SECOND EDITION

 WORLD BOOK

a Scott Fetzer company
Chicago
www.worldbookonline.com

J

Contents

NEPTUNE

If a word is printed in **bold letters that look like this,** that word's meaning is given in the glossary on page 63.

THE DISTANT DWARF PLANETS

Where Is Neptune?

Neptune is the eighth and most distant **planet** from the sun. Neptune's **orbit** lies between the orbits of Uranus (*YUR uh nuhs* or *yu RAY nuhs*), its inner neighbor, and Pluto, the **dwarf planet** that is Neptune's outer neighbor. Once about every 250 years, however, Pluto's **elliptical** orbit dips inside Neptune's orbit for a span of about 20 years. This change in position between Neptune and Pluto last happened from January 1979 to February 1999.

Neptune's average distance from the sun is about 2.8 billion miles (4.5 billion kilometers). That's about 30 times farther from the sun than Earth is.

Neptune is one of the planets in our **solar system** that **astronomers** call the outer planets. The other outer planets are Jupiter, Saturn, and Uranus.

Planet Locator

Note: The size of the sun and planets and the distance between planets in this diagram are not to scale.

Neptune

Uranus

Saturn

Jupiter

Mars

Earth

Venus

Mercury

Sun

Neptune's symbol (top left) and a diagram showing the planet's location in the solar system

How Big Is Neptune?

Neptune is the fourth-largest **planet** in our **solar system.** Only Jupiter, Saturn, and Uranus are larger. However, Uranus is only slightly larger than Neptune. If the planets were side by side, you would have to look closely to see there is a difference in size.

The **diameter** of Neptune at its **equator** is 30,775 miles (49,528 kilometers). That is nearly four times the diameter of Earth. Next to Earth, Neptune would look like a giant planet. If Neptune were hollow, it would take about 58 planets the size of Earth to fill it up.

An artist's drawing comparing the size of Neptune and Earth

Neptune's diameter
30,775 miles
(49,528 kilometers)

Earth's diameter
7,926 miles
(12,756 kilometers)

What Does Neptune Look Like?

Neptune is far from Earth—so far that we cannot see it in the sky without a telescope. But when seen through a telescope, Neptune appears as a bright point in the sky, like a star.

When photographed from space by a **probe,** Neptune looks like a giant blue ball with tiny wisps of white clouds. The planet has a belt of six rings around its middle, but the rings are so faint that they do not show up in most photographs. Neptune's bright blue color is caused by **methane** gas at the top of its **atmosphere.**

Neptune's high, thin, streaky white clouds look like clouds on Earth that are called cirrus clouds. Cirrus clouds are made of ice crystals that form very high in Earth's atmosphere.

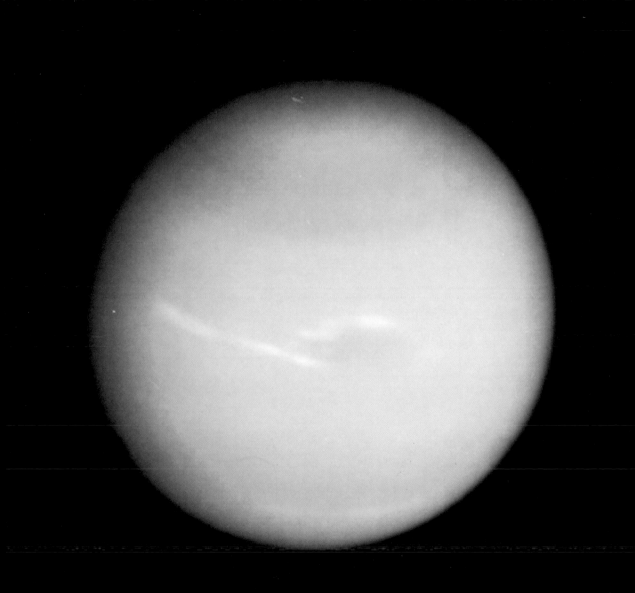

Neptune in a
natural-color photo

What Makes Up Neptune?

Scientists label the four largest **planets** in the **solar system** the **gas giants.** These planets are Jupiter, Saturn, Uranus, and Neptune. All these planets are made up of large amounts of gas and liquid.

Scientists believe that Neptune is a huge ball of highly pressurized gas and liquid. They think that Neptune is made up mostly of **hydrogen, helium,** water, and **silicates.** Unlike Earth, Neptune has no solid ground.

The part of Neptune that we can see consists of several cloud layers. Deeper in, there is a layer of compressed gases—mostly hydrogen and helium gases. Farther inside the planet, in the layer known as the **mantle,** the gases blend into a layer of liquid. Some scientists think that this layer of liquid might be superheated water that would boil away if it could, but the **pressure** of the surrounding gases keeps it from doing so. Inside the mantle is most likely a solid **core** made of ice and rock.

The Interior of Neptune

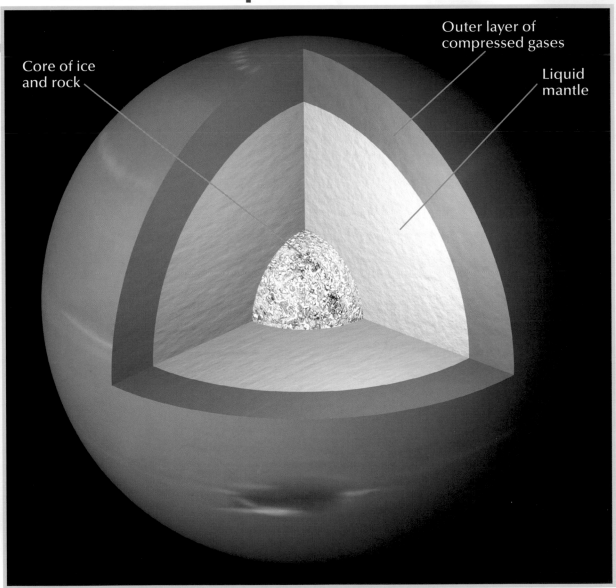

Core of ice and rock

Outer layer of compressed gases

Liquid mantle

What Is Neptune's Atmosphere Like?

Neptune is surrounded by thick layers of clouds. The **atmosphere** of Neptune seems to be layered. Clouds made up mainly of **methane** surround Neptune and give the planet its blue color. The clouds farthest from Neptune's surface consist mainly of frozen methane.

Darker cloud layers deeper inside Neptune seem to be made of **hydrogen sulfide.** This colorless gas has the odor of rotten eggs and, at high levels, it can be dangerous or even deadly to humans. Neptune's atmosphere also contains **hydrogen** and **helium.**

Clouds on Neptune in a natural-color photo

What Is the Weather on Neptune?

The weather on Neptune is cloudy, windy, and cold! The average temperature of Neptune's outer cloud layer is −355 °F (−215 °C).

Neptune is a world of violent winds. These fierce winds blow at speeds as high as 900 miles (1,450 kilometers) per hour! Earth's strongest winds blow only about one-third that speed. The winds of Neptune blow the thick cloud layers around that planet very fast.

Scientists have found evidence of changing seasons on Neptune. The tilt of Neptune's **axis** is similar to the tilt of Earth's axis, so Neptune has four seasons, as does Earth. When scientists recently studied photographs of the planet taken over a span of several years, they found that clouds in the southern half of Neptune have become much brighter—evidence that it is now spring on that part of the planet. On Neptune, one season is not, as on Earth, three months long—instead, it lasts for more than 40 years! Spring may last for around another 20 years on Neptune.

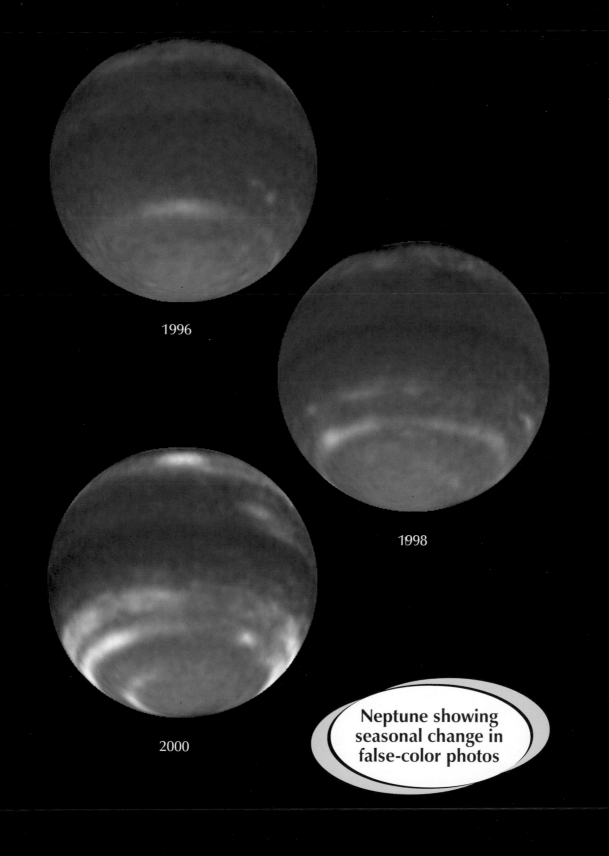

1996

1998

2000

Neptune showing
seasonal change in
false-color photos

How Does Neptune Compare with Earth?

Although Neptune has about 17 times more **mass** than Earth, its average **density** is only about 1.5 times that of Earth's. Neptune's surface **gravity** is slightly greater than Earth's. If you weighed 100 pounds on Earth, you would weigh about 112 pounds on Neptune.

Earth is close enough to the light-giving sun to absorb much of that heat and keep out the frigid conditions of space. But Neptune is on the outer fringes of our **solar system.** It receives a tiny fraction of the sunlight that bathes Earth. If you could view the sun from Neptune, it would look 900 times dimmer than here on our Earth.

How Do They Compare?

	Earth ⊕	Neptune ♆
Size in diameter (at equator)	7,926 miles (12,756 kilometers)	30,775 miles (49,528 kilometers)
Average distance from sun	About 93 million miles (150 million kilometers)	About 2.8 billion miles (4.5 billion kilometers)
Length of year (in Earth days)	365.256	60,189
Length of day (in Earth time)	24 hours	16 hours 7 minutes
What an object would weigh…	If it weighed 100 pounds on Earth…	…it would weigh about 112 pounds on Neptune.
Number of moons	1	At least 13
Rings?	No	Yes
Atmosphere	Nitrogen, oxygen, argon	Hydrogen, helium, methane, acetylene

What Are the Orbit and Rotation of Neptune Like?

Like the other **planets** in our **solar system,** Neptune travels in an **orbit** around the sun that is **elliptical.** However, Neptune's orbit is more nearly round than the orbits of all the other planets except Venus.

On average, Neptune is about 2.8 billion miles (4.5 billion kilometers) from the sun. Because the planet is so very far from the sun, it takes Neptune about 165 Earth years to complete one orbit. In fact, in the time since Neptune was first discovered by **astronomers** in the mid-1800's, the planet has not yet completed one orbit. It will do so in 2011. With a **year** that is around 165 Earth years long, New Year's celebrations would be few and far between on Neptune!

Neptune rotates (spins around) on its **axis,** making one complete turn, or rotation, every 16 hours and 7 minutes in Earth time. That's the length of a **day** on Neptune.

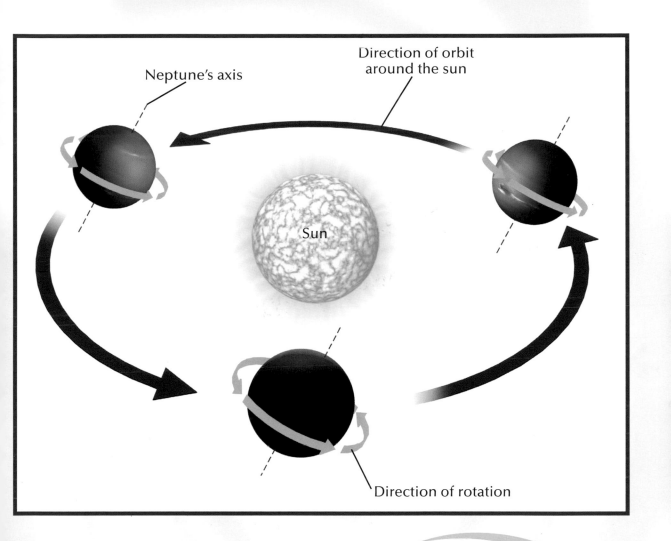

Neptune's axis

Direction of orbit around the sun

Sun

Direction of rotation

A diagram showing the orbit and rotation of Neptune

What Makes Up Neptune's Rings?

Like the other **gas giants** in our **solar system,** Neptune has a system of rings. Scientists have counted six rings circling the planet's **equator.**

Neptune's rings are probably made of dust and are very faint, but three arcs, or sections, of the outer ring shine more brightly than other parts of the ring. Scientists believe that dust may be concentrated more thickly in these bright sections. One of Neptune's **moons,** Galatea *(gal uh TEE uh),* **orbits** the **planet** just inside the outer ring. The pull of its **gravity** probably concentrates dust in the three bright arcs.

We did not know anything about rings on Neptune until the 1980's, when **astronomers** watched the planet pass in front of a star. The starlight "winked" when it crossed a ring. The Voyager 2 **probe**—launched by the National Aeronautics and Space Administration (NASA) in 1977—confirmed the existence of the rings in 1989.

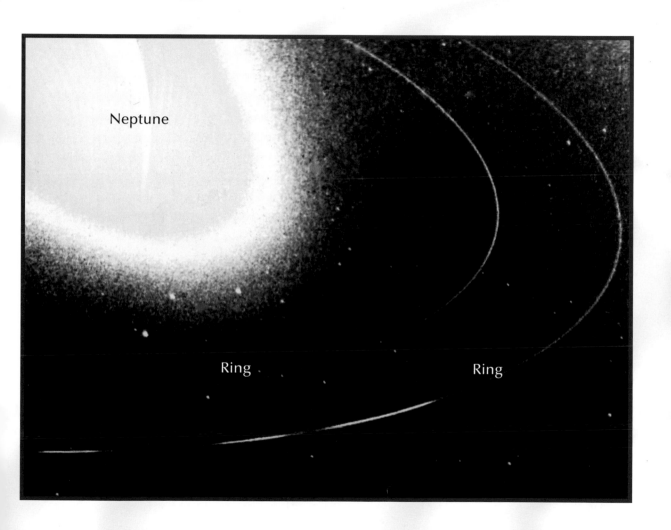

Neptune

Ring   Ring

How Many Moons Does Neptune Have?

Neptune has at least 13 **moons.** The three largest moons are Triton *(TRY tuhn),* Proteus *(PROH tee uhs),* and Nereid *(NIHR ee ihd).* Triton is one of the larger moons in our **solar system,** but Neptune's other moons are quite small.

Proteus, Neptune's second-largest moon, is dark and quite close to the planet. **Astronomers** using telescopes on Earth overlooked this small moon, but images sent by Voyager 2 when it visited Neptune in 1989 allowed scientists to discover Proteus. Nereid, Neptune's third-largest moon, has an **orbit** that is the most **elliptical** of any moon in the solar system. Proteus, Nereid, and Neptune's other small moons are all less than 300 miles (480 kilometers) in **diameter.**

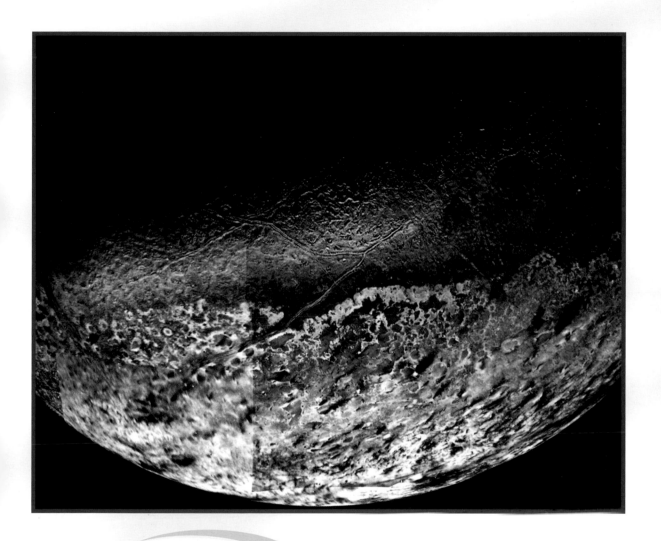

Neptune's moon Triton in
a natural-color photo

What Is Unusual About Neptune's Moon Triton?

Triton, which is Neptune's largest **moon,** has a **diameter** of about 1,680 miles (2,700 kilometers). It is one of the larger moons in our **solar system.** Only Jupiter's four largest moons, Earth's moon, and Saturn's moon Titan are larger.

Like Saturn's Titan—and unlike most other moons—Triton has an **atmosphere.** It is made mainly of **nitrogen** gas. Triton has **geysers**—streams of nitrogen and other material that spurt occasionally from below its surface. Triton is the coldest body in the solar system, with a surface temperature of about –390 °F (–235 °C).

Triton **orbits** Neptune in the direction opposite to Neptune's rotation. That's why scientists think Triton was captured by Neptune's **gravity** long after Neptune formed. Triton's orbit is gradually dropping closer to Neptune. Millions of years from now, it may break up and form a new ring around Neptune.

An artist's drawing imagining the surface of Triton, with Neptune in the background

How Did Neptune Get Its Name?

People in ancient times knew nothing about the **planet** Neptune. In the 1800's, several **astronomers** noticed an unusual movement in the **orbit** of the planet Uranus and predicted the existence of another planet orbiting beyond Uranus. German astronomer Johann G. Galle *(GAHL uh)* and his assistant, Heinrich L. d'Arrest *(duh REST),* first viewed the planet we now know as Neptune through a telescope in 1846. However, the scientists who had correctly predicted Neptune's location—John C. Adams of England and Urbain J. J. Leverrier *(luh VEHR ee ay)* of France—are given credit for the discovery.

The scientists named the new planet for Neptune, the Roman god of the sea. The name fits well, for the planet looks blue, like a lake or sea. Neptune's **moons** are also named for mythical sea beings. Triton, for example, was the name the ancient Greeks used for a sea god in the form of a merman—a humanlike creature with the tail and lower body of a fish.

The symbol for the planet Neptune (see page 7) is a three-pronged spear that the god is said to have carried.

What Space Missions Have Studied Neptune?

A **probe** from NASA's Voyager missions, Voyager 2, was launched from Earth in 1977. On August 25, 1989, the Voyager 2 probe passed within about 3,000 miles (4,850 kilometers) of the cloud-covered surface of Neptune. That was 3½ years after the probe's **fly-by** of Uranus, exactly 8 years after the probe's visit to Saturn, and 10 years after its Jupiter encounter.

Voyager 2 sent a large amount of information about Neptune back to Earth, which greatly expanded our knowledge about that planet. The probe found six new **moons** around Neptune. Previously, only two—Triton and Nereid—had been known. Voyager 2 also increased **astronomers'** limited knowledge of Neptune's faint rings.

Voyager 2 data also revealed much about Triton, Neptune's largest and most interesting moon. The probe returned photographs showing **geysers** spurting **nitrogen** gas and dust into Triton's thin **atmosphere.**

An artist's drawing of
Voyager 2

Could There Be Life on Neptune or Its Moons?

Scientists believe there is very little chance of finding any kind of life on Neptune or its **moons.** Neptune's **atmosphere** is made up of gases that would be quite poisonous if breathed by most of the living things we know about. And, the temperature at the cloudtops is an incredibly frigid –355 °F (–215 °C)!

Deep inside Neptune, there may be an ocean of water, but if so, it is probably boiling hot. And the **pressure** inside Neptune may be great enough to crush spaceships, much less living things.

Neptune's only large moon with any atmosphere is Triton. But it is very hard to imagine any kind of life that could exist at such extremely cold temperatures. The most frigid places on Earth at Antarctica would seem warm and inviting compared to Triton.

There may be life somewhere in the universe other than on Earth. But it is not likely to be found on or near Neptune.

Neptune (top) and Triton
in a false-color photo

What Are the Distant Dwarf Planets?

There are icy objects beyond the **orbit** of Neptune that seem larger than **comets** or **asteroids,** but they are not quite big enough to be **planets.** A group of **astronomers** called the International Astronomical Union (IAU) created the term **dwarf planet** to describe these objects. The distant dwarf planets include Pluto and Eris (*IHR his* or *EHR his*), but other objects in the same region have the necessary traits to be dwarf planets.

According to the IAU, an object needs to have three traits to be considered a dwarf planet. It must be round, orbit the sun, and have so little **gravity** that it is not able to clear other objects from its orbit.

Until August 2006, Pluto was considered a planet, but some astronomers had always questioned this. In 2005, when scientists announced the discovery of an object larger than Pluto orbiting beyond Pluto's orbit, it created even more doubt about Pluto's status. For a short time, it seemed that the larger object, named Eris in 2006, might become the 10th planet of our **solar system.** Instead, the IAU chose to reduce the number of planets from 9 to 8. Despite some controversy, Pluto became a dwarf planet, along with Eris.

An artist's drawing shows a dim sun (left) and moon (right) from the surface of Pluto, a distant dwarf planet

Where Are the Distant Dwarf Planets?

There is a wide region at the edge of our **solar system** called the **Kuiper** *(KY pur)* **belt.** The belt is named after the Dutch-born American **astronomer,** Gerard P. Kuiper (1905–1973), who described this region.

The Kuiper belt begins beyond the **orbit** of Neptune, on average about 2.8 billion miles (4.5 billion kilometers) from the sun. The Kuiper belt's outer edge is about 4.6 billion miles (7.5 billion kilometers) from the sun. The belt is a doughnut-shaped band made up of many small- to medium-sized objects called Kuiper belt objects—or KBO's. At this cold and distant edge of the solar system are the distant **dwarf planets,** including Pluto and Eris.

Pluto was the first large object discovered in this region. Not until 1992 did astronomers begin to find other Kuiper belt objects. We now realize that the outer solar system contains a large number of these rocky, icy objects. Some are round and could be classed as dwarf planets. Most of the smaller objects are not round and will continue to be called Kuiper belt objects. Pluto and Eris are both Kuiper belt objects and dwarf planets.

Note: Neither the size of objects nor the distance between objects in this diagram are to scale.

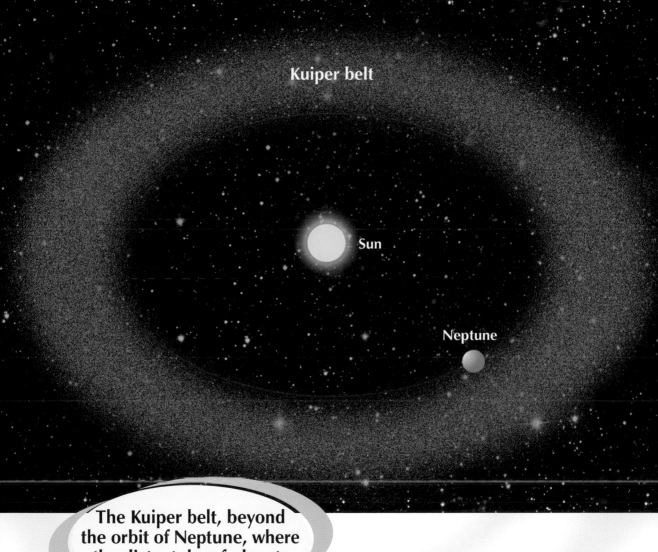

Kuiper belt

Sun

Neptune

The Kuiper belt, beyond the orbit of Neptune, where the distant dwarf planets are found

How Big Are the Distant Dwarf Planets?

Pluto is the best-known **dwarf planet.** But, with a **diameter** of about 1,400 miles (2,300 kilometers), it is not the largest dwarf planet.

The largest dwarf planet we know of is Eris. Eris is about 1,500 miles (2,400 kilometers) in diameter.

It is not certain which object in the **Kuiper belt** is the smallest dwarf planet, but there is a limit on how small an object can be and still be a dwarf planet. That is because a dwarf planet must have a round shape, and what makes an object in space round is the **gravity** of the object itself. An object's own gravity pulls downward at its surface. With enough gravity, the object's surface eventually takes the shape of a ball.

For objects made of rock and ice, like Kuiper belt objects, the smallest an object could be and still be round would likely be around 185 miles (300 kilometers) in diameter.

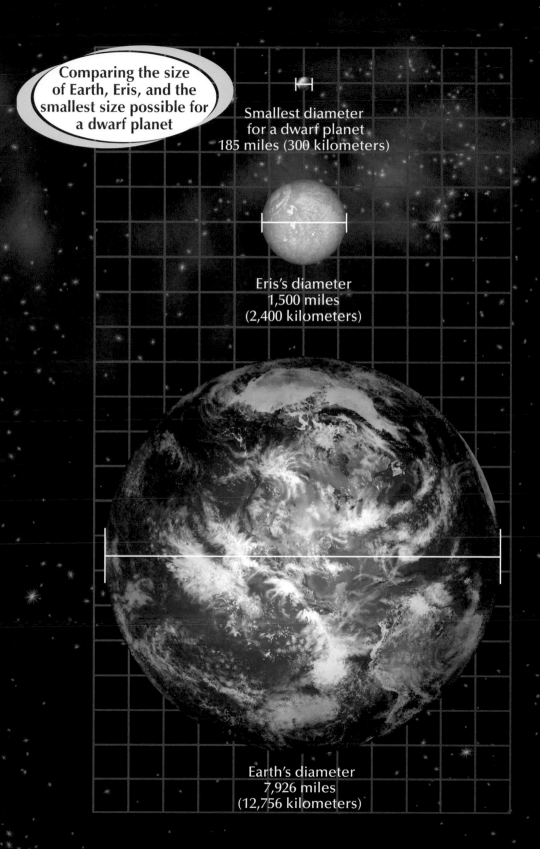

Comparing the size of Earth, Eris, and the smallest size possible for a dwarf planet

Smallest diameter for a dwarf planet
185 miles (300 kilometers)

Eris's diameter
1,500 miles
(2,400 kilometers)

Earth's diameter
7,926 miles
(12,756 kilometers)

What Makes Up the Distant Dwarf Planets?

All of the distant **dwarf planets** are most likely made up of ice and rock in varying combinations. The dwarf planet we know most about is Pluto, and since Pluto is not likely to be completely different from the other distant dwarf planets, we can use it as an example.

Even though Pluto is the dwarf planet we know best, it is so far away and we have so little scientific data about it, scientists can only make educated guesses about its make up. Scientists know that Pluto has less **density** than Earth. That means the matter that makes up Pluto is packed much less tightly than Earth's matter is.

Scientists think most of Pluto is made of water ice. In contrast, most of Earth is made of rock. Pluto may have a **core** of solid rock and some metals, but this is likely surrounded by a thick layer of water ice. If so, that would explain why Earth has more density than Pluto does. Rock is more dense than water, which is why a rock sinks in water. Ice is less dense than water, and that is why icebergs float on water. So, if Earth were much rockier than Pluto was, that would explain the difference in density between the two.

The Interior of Pluto

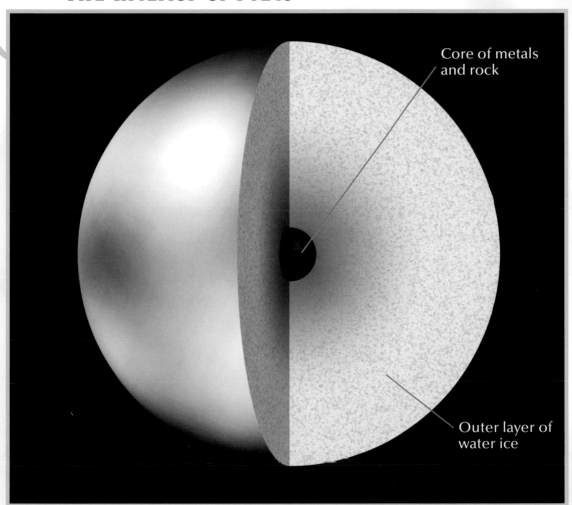

Core of metals and rock

Outer layer of water ice

What Does Pluto Look Like?

Pluto is really far away. The closest it ever gets to Earth is about 2.7 billion miles (4.3 billion kilometers). That is so distant that Pluto looks like a blurry disk through even the most powerful Earth-based telescopes.

From what **astronomers** have been able to gather from such tools as the Hubble Space Telescope, Pluto appears to have a brownish color. It has bright splotches that are probably **polar caps.** Astronomers can also make out dark spots scattered across Pluto's surface.

Scientists have learned that Pluto has a thin **atmosphere.** That atmosphere is made up mostly of **nitrogen** gas and is similar to the atmosphere on Neptune's **moon** Triton. Astronomers do not know if the atmosphere on Pluto features any visible clouds or hazes, so it is not certain that the atmosphere affects the look of Pluto, as the atmospheres of Jupiter and Earth affect their appearance. Observations made in 2002, however, do allow scientists to know that the atmosphere of Pluto is expanding (growing larger).

An artist's drawing
of Pluto

What Are the Orbit and Rotation of Pluto Like?

For a **planet,** Pluto's **orbit** would be unusual. Pluto's orbit around the sun is much more **elliptical** than the orbits of the eight planets of the **solar system.** Further, all the planets orbit fairly closely within one plane. Imagine that you had eight balls circling around on a plate; the eight planets orbiting the sun are somewhat like that. But, the orbit of Pluto is tilted in respect to that orbital plane, called the ecliptic. For some parts of Pluto's orbit, it is high above the ecliptic, and for other parts it is below. An orbit like this makes more sense for a **Kuiper belt** object than a planet. In fact, Pluto's odd orbit was one of the reasons some **astronomers** began to feel it could not be a planet.

The orbit of Pluto takes a very long time. Pluto is so far from the sun that it takes about 248 Earth years to go around the sun once. That's one **year** on Pluto. For about 20 Earth years out of that 248-year orbit time, Pluto dips inside the orbit of Neptune. That happened last between 1979 and 1999. It will not happen again until the 2200's.

Pluto rotates (spins around) on its **axis** about one time every six Earth **days.** So, a day on Pluto lasts for a long time!

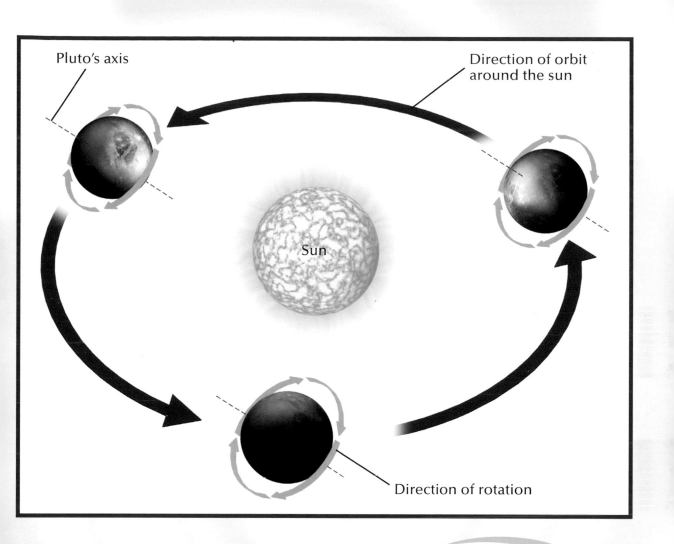

Pluto's axis

Direction of orbit
around the sun

Sun

Direction of rotation

A diagram showing
the orbit and rotation
of Pluto

How Many Moons Does Pluto Have?

Pluto has three **moons.** Pluto's largest and best-known moon is Charon *(KAR uhn* or *KAY rohn)*. Pluto also has two smaller moons named Nix *(nihks)* and Hydra *(HY druh)*. Charon's **orbit** is closest to Pluto. The next moon out is Nix, and the orbit of Hydra is furthest out from Pluto.

Charon is about half the size of Pluto. In our **solar system**, it is quite unusual for an object to have a moon so large. Also, Pluto and Charon are very close to each other in distance—only about 12,200 miles (19,600 kilometers) apart. Scientists think that Charon's surface is covered by dirty water ice. Charon's surface is much less reflective, or shiny, than Pluto's surface, and it does not have contrasting bright and dark spots like Pluto. And, unlike Pluto, Charon does not have an **atmosphere.**

In October 2005, NASA announced that the Hubble Space Telescope had sent images of two new moons of Pluto. In 2006, the International Astronomical Union (IAU) gave these moons the names Nix and Hydra. These small moons are two to three times as far from Pluto as Charon is and are much smaller than Charon.

Pluto

Nix

Hydra

Charon

Pluto and its three moons, Charon, Nix, and Hydra

Who Discovered Pluto?

American **astronomer** Clyde W. Tombaugh (*TOM baw*, 1906-1997) discovered Pluto in 1930 while at the Lowell Observatory in Flagstaff, Arizona.

Pluto was considered a **planet** after Tombaugh discovered it, but its status was changed to **dwarf planet** in 2006. This does not really change the importance of Tombaugh's discovery, however. He was the first to discover an object belonging to what scientists consider to be the "third group" from the sun. The first group is made up of the inner planets—Mercury, Venus, Earth, and Mars, which are rocky. The second group is made up of the outer planets—Jupiter, Saturn, Uranus, and Neptune, which are **gas giants.** Then there is a group of icy dwarf planets and **Kuiper belt** objects far from the sun. It could be that Pluto is best placed in this group, and Tombaugh found its first member.

To honor Tombaugh and his discovery, a small canister holding some of his cremated (burned) remains was placed on the New Horizons spacecraft (see page 50) that was launched in 2006. This spacecraft should fly past Pluto in 2015 and will continue out into the Kuiper belt.

Clyde Tombaugh

Is There a Space Mission Planned to Study Pluto?

There is still a lot we do not know about Pluto. Our best telescopes on Earth can produce only small, blurry images of the **dwarf planet.** That's one reason why, in the early 2000's, NASA began planning the New Horizons space mission to Pluto, Charon, and the **Kuiper belt**.

The New Horizons spacecraft weighs about 1,000 pounds (about 450 kilograms) and is about the size of a grand piano. It is loaded with scientific instruments that can take pictures and temperatures, analyze chemicals, and make surface maps, among many other things.

The New Horizons spacecraft launched in January 2006. It is on a one-way journey and should reach Pluto and Charon in 2015. Students who were in first grade when the spacecraft blasted off will be in high school when New Horizons starts sending pictures back from Pluto!

What Does Eris Look Like?

Eris is a distant **dwarf planet** well beyond the **orbit** of Pluto. It is made up of ice and rock. In that sense, Eris probably looks something like Pluto. There are, however, differences between these dwarf planets.

Pluto is thought to be brownish in color with bright and dark splotches. But Eris is white and has a uniform appearance.

There is another way that Eris is different from Pluto. Eris is very shiny. That is, it reflects much of the light that hits it back out again, as a mirror would. Eris reflects about 85 percent of the sunlight that hits it. By comparison, Pluto reflects about 60 percent. There is only one known object in the **solar system** with a brighter surface than Eris. That is Saturn's **moon** Enceladus, which reflects almost 100 percent of the light that reaches it.

Scientists have a guess as to why Eris is so white and shiny. They think Eris may have a thin **atmosphere** made up of **methane**. If so, because Eris is so far from the sun, such an atmosphere would be frozen solid. This frozen atmosphere could form a reflective sheet of ice.

An artist's drawing of
Eris and its moon,
Dysnomia

What Are the Orbit and Rotation of Eris Like?

Eris is the farthest object we have ever found orbiting the sun. The **orbit** of Eris is on average around 6.3 billion miles (10.1 billion kilometers) from the sun. The average distance of Pluto's orbit is 3.6 billion miles (5.9 billion kilometers) from the sun.

The orbit of Eris is very different from the almost circular orbits of the **planets.** The orbit of Eris is very **elliptical**. At its closest distance from the sun, Eris is 3.5 billion miles (5.7 billion kilometers) away. When it is at its furthest point from the sun, Eris is 9 billion miles (14.5 billion kilometers) away. Eris also has a very tilted orbit. (See page 44 for information on Pluto's tilted orbit.)

It takes Eris a very long time to orbit the sun—560 Earth years. That's the length of one **year** on Eris.

We do not know anything about the rotation of Eris. For **astronomers** to know about an object's rotation, there needs to be something that causes the object to look different as it spins—something such as a dark patch or a spot that appears to move as the object rotates. Eris appears as a uniform, white, shining ball. For now, there is nothing to allow astronomers to see its rotation.

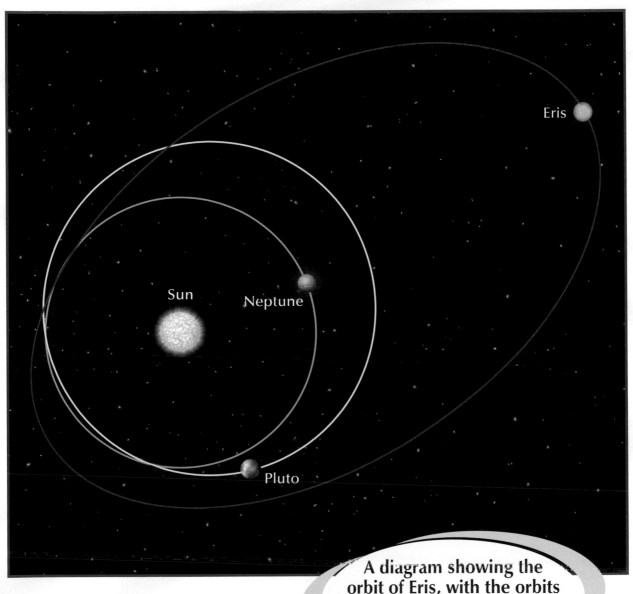

A diagram showing the orbit of Eris, with the orbits of Neptune and Pluto included for comparison

How Many Moons Does Eris Have?

Astronomers were excited to discover that Eris has one **moon.** It was discovered in September 2005. In 2006, that moon was named Dysnomia (*dihs NOH mee uh*).

That may seem like an odd name for a moon, but it is a very appropriate name for a moon orbiting Eris. In ancient Greek religion, Eris was the goddess of discord (disagreement). In one well-known myth about Eris, she tossed a golden apple, called the Apple of Discord, among three goddesses. The apple was engraved with the phrase, "For the fairest." Each of these goddesses began arguing and scheming to ensure that the apple was awarded to her. Eris seems like a good name for a **dwarf planet** that created such discord among astronomers about which objects in the **solar system** are **planets.**

Now that you know a little about the name Eris, the name Dysnomia will make more sense. Moons are usually named for something that is associated with the name or the qualities of the object they **orbit.** Eris's moon was named for the goddess of discord's daughter, Dysnomia. Dysnomia is a Greek word that means "lawlessness."

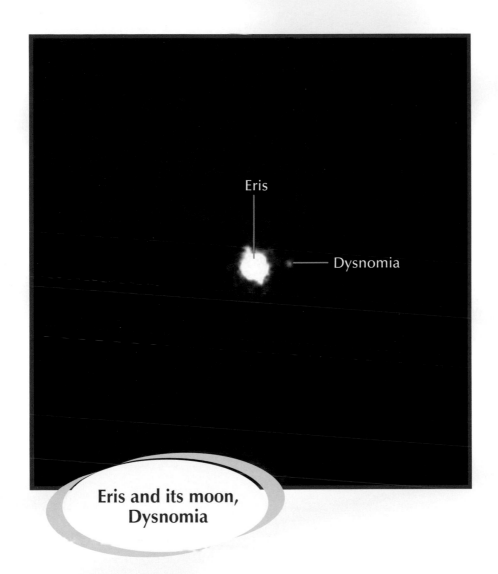

Eris and its moon, Dysnomia

Who Discovered Eris?

   Three **astronomers** discovered Eris—Michael (Mike) Brown (1965–   ), Chadwick (Chad) Trujillo (1973–   ), and David Rabinowitz (1960–   ). These astronomers have found many distant objects in the **solar system,** including a number of objects large enough to be considered **dwarf planets.**

   Brown, Trujillo, and Rabinowitz find these objects by studying photos of a small area of the sky taken at different times. Nonmoving objects such as stars will appear the same in the photos, but **planets, dwarf planets, asteroids,** and other objects that move will appear in a different place on each photo. Clyde Tombaugh (see page 48) used much the same method to discover Pluto. Brown's team, however, can use computers to help them find the moving objects.

   In January 2005, a review of photos taken in 2003 turned up a distant object moving as a planet or asteroid would. The find was verified and later announced by the team in 2005 and was given the temporary designation of 2003 UB313. Brown nicknamed the object Xena *(Zee nah).* Once the International Astronomical Union (IAU) decided that the object was a dwarf planet in 2006, it was given the name Eris.

Astronomers Mike Brown (top left), Chad Trujillo (top right), and David Rabinowitz (left)

Could There Be Other Distant Dwarf Planets?

In the inner **solar system**, the only **dwarf planet** is Ceres, a large **asteroid** between the **orbits** of Mars and Jupiter. It is the only object large enough to be round that is not a full **planet** in the inner solar system.

The resolution (official decision) passed by the International Astronomical Union (IAU) mentioned only two dwarf planets in the outer solar system: Eris and Pluto. However, there are a number of round objects in this region that fit the definition for a dwarf planet, including Sedna *(SEHD nuh)* and Quaoar *(KWAH oh wahr)*. Sedna, discovered in 2004, measures about three-fourths the size of Pluto. Quaoar, discovered in 2002, measures roughly half the size of Pluto. These are two of dozens of objects discovered beyond the orbit of Neptune that currently fit the IAU definition for a dwarf planet.

Of course, in the far-off **Kuiper belt** and beyond, where the distant dwarf planets are found, we have only begun to survey the sky. Mike Brown has estimated that once the Kuiper belt is fully mapped, the number of dwarf planets it contains could be more than 200.

An artist's conception
of the Kuiper belt

FUN FACTS About NEPTUNE & the DISTANT DWARF PLANETS

★ Triton, Neptune's largest **moon,** was discovered only three weeks after the **planet** itself, in 1846.

★ Gerard P. Kuiper, the **astronomer** for whom the **Kuiper belt** was named, discovered Neptune's moon Nereid in 1949. It was the first moon of Neptune to be discovered in 103 years.

★ Sunlight on Neptune is 900 times dimmer than on Earth, yet Neptune has violent weather. Scientists are not really sure why—they would predict that a planet that receives so little of the sun's energy should have much less active weather.

★ Pluto is so small that the **dwarf planet** would cover only about half the width of the United States.

★ Modern astronomy is different from the stargazing of earlier times. The astronomers who discovered Eris work far from one another—Mike Brown in Pasadena, California; Chad Trujillo in Hawaii; and David Rabinowitz in Connecticut. Further, the telescope they use is at the Palomar Observatory in San Diego, California. Astronomers no longer peer through a telescope to see images of distant objects. They now look at those objects on a computer screen, and that computer can be thousands of miles from their telescope.

Glossary

asteroid A small body made of rock, carbon, or metal that orbits the sun. Most asteroids are between the orbits of Mars and Jupiter.

astronomer A scientist who studies stars and planets.

atmosphere The mass of gases that surrounds a planet.

axis In planets, the imaginary line about which the planet seems to turn, or rotate. (The axis of Earth is an imaginary line through the North Pole and the South Pole.)

carbon monoxide A compound formed of carbon and oxygen.

comet A small body made of dirt and ice that orbits the sun.

core The center part of the inside of a planet.

day The time it takes a planet to rotate (spin) once around its axis and come back to the same position in relation to the sun.

density The amount of matter in a given space.

diameter The distance of a straight line through the middle of a circle or a thing shaped like a ball.

dwarf planet A round body in space orbiting a star, which does not have enough gravitational pull to clear other objects from its orbit.

elliptical Having the shape of an ellipse, which is like an oval or flattened circle.

equator An imaginary circle around the middle of a planet.

fly-by The flight of a space vehicle close to a planet or body in space.

gas giant Any of four planets—Jupiter, Saturn, Uranus, and Neptune—made up mostly of gas and liquid.

geyser A stream that from time to time spurts hot water or gases and other material with explosive force.

gravity The effect of a force of attraction that acts between all objects because of their mass (that is, the amount of matter the objects have).

helium The second most abundant chemical element in the universe.

hydrogen The most abundant chemical element in the universe.

hydrogen sulfide A compound formed of hydrogen and sulfur.

Kuiper belt A ring of small objects orbiting in the outer solar system beyond Neptune. Scientists believe that many comets are objects from the Kuiper belt.

mantle The area of a planet between the crust and the core.

mass The amount of matter a thing contains.

methane A compound formed of the chemical elements carbon and hydrogen.

moon A smaller body that orbits a planet.

nitrogen A nonmetallic chemical element.

orbit The path that a smaller body takes around a larger body, for instance, the path that a planet takes around the sun. Also, to travel in an orbit.

planet A large, round body in space that orbits a star. A planet must have sufficient gravitational pull to clear other objects from the area of its orbit.

polar cap A white or bright area on the poles of some planets, including Mars and Pluto, that resembles ice or snow.

pressure The force caused by the weight of a planet's atmosphere as it presses down on the layers below it.

probe An unpiloted device sent to explore space. Most probes send data (information) from space.

silicate One of a group of minerals that contain silicon, oxygen, and one or more metallic elements.

solar system A group of bodies in space made up of a star and the planets and other objects orbiting around that star.

year The time it takes a planet to complete one orbit around the sun.

Index

For more information about Neptune and the distant dwarf planets, try these resources:

The Far Planets by Robin Kerrod, Raintree, 2002

Neptune:
A Look at Neptune, by John Tabak, Franklin Watts, 2003

Neptune, by Carmen Bredeson, Franklin Watts, 2003

Neptune, by Seymour Simon, Sagebrush, 1999

Neptune:
http://nssdc.gsfc.nasa.gov/planetary/planets/neptunepage.html
http://www.windows.ucar.edu/tour/link=/neptune/neptune.html
Pluto:
http://nssdc.gsfc.nasa.gov/planetary/planets/plutopage.html
http://pluto.jhuapl.edu/
Eris:
http://www.gps.caltech.edu/~mbrown/planetlila/